LifeGoodenergy  Affirmations

WELCOME

Welcome on this Journey!! If you want to get a little comfortable take a seat, but for you to be reading this book, you already took a stand. I'm grateful for your attendance and support on exploring each other minds on our similar goals but separate paths. The goal is to keep the mind thinking with thoughts that remind you of your greatness and lead you to your throne. Never fail to question other people's thoughts, but you must remember they are just other people's thoughts. There will be times to cry, times to laugh, times to sigh, and times you just disagree. But remember, they can all be Good Times because the time can be to change, the time can be for on the right path remembrance, the time can be to teach, or the time to learn. It's all based on where you're at in your life and where you're planning on going. I encourage you to be always open-minded and not be quick to judge others. You have to understand everybody thinking, learning, and applying abilities are totally different. And anyone who knows better brings no harms. Let's enjoy the peace of everything; even if you think you don't have the piece of anything. You will always have, You, the best gift ever. And you must know your presence brings presents.

INTRODUCTION

L et the journey continue, as we headed for greatness beyond your imagination. You have made the decision that you want to be reminded of all the small positive things that can bring a big difference in your life. It all starts in the morning right after you awake from a nightmare of fears or a dream of happiness and peace. The decision you must quickly make determines the rest of your day. Then you realize the rest of days end up being your life forever. You want to take the time to fellowship, thank, and praise your higher power, if you have one. And continue to let the power of all good things flow in you. Because you are in so much control of everything that comes your way, so take the advantage of seeing everything as half full instead of half empty. The discouragement and failure are waiting on you to open a door, to stop all possibilities of you being success in your own way. The crazy part is that they only hurt you when you do not allow yourself to see it as help. It brings an opportunity of growth for you and allow you to understand how much more of positivity you need around you at all times. Never fail to have a caring family and friends, motivation material, spiritual information, and any other thing you can have around to keep you positive. But here in this book we have something real special for you. We have affirmations that are here to keep you focus each and every day. I personally use them daily myself and encourage others to do so as well. May your Greatness be found and keep in front of you, as you put behind [All] that wants to destroy you. You Got This! I will always be around cheering you on. You are strong! You are real! You are ready! Let's Go!!

You can't outgrow friends, that are growing with you.

You are the seed, let your storms be the water, and let your light shine.

Never let them misdiagnose you as, Not being Successful, only you know that.

If you don't know your weaknesses, then how will you know if you have grown.

When I hurt I hurt, but when I heal, I really heal!

Small talks and small walks bring big differences in every journey.

Don't doubt the symptoms, if you don't want it to crash your system.

You not in the race, you are the race, you are in your own race.

You don't want to be the victim of what you can't do, you want to be a victor of what you can do.

The question is not who is on your team, the question is, who doing their part to be called the team.

The only reason people are negative because they stop drawing the line to be positive.

I *rather not have enough time to do everything, than to have enough time to do nothing.*

A person having more than
enough information and doing
nothing with it, is worse than
person just having a lack of
information.

You must be willing to travel roads that People usually detour from.

You can consider yourself a great person if you can pick up great things from great people.

You can play weak all you want, but if you pray for strength, you have to show it.

You're loose, Not broken!

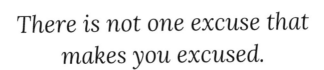

There is not one excuse that
makes you excused.

Never ask a quitter how to win.

The only thing that you can be the best at, IS YOU, everything else is debatable.

You can dream anything, but
making it reality is everything.

You haven't failed when you are falling, you have failed when you don't get up.

Your beauty makes other see more beauty.

Your gifts bring gifts and your presence bring presents.

The world sees the image of what you imagine when your dreams becomes reality.

Great jewels create more gems!

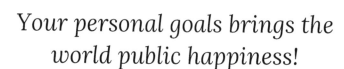

Your personal goals brings the world public happiness!

I no longer meet friends in my life
I usually hang around
journeymen!

Prayers can be with you, but faith must be in you!

You can be whoever you want to be, I am LifeGoodenergy!

I WANNA THANK YOU !

There are so many days when people just need a word of hope, of care, of desire, or well-being. We all have fire in us, but when we get that fuel, it feels totally different than usual. The burden is lifted, and the fears are vanished. And everything seems so easily possible and done. It feels like, I can fly, some would say to me. Seeing that joy in others bring me so much peace to myself. The reason is that the more people that can catch a fire, can then light themselves, and next is lighting others. Then we start to build a whole community of beautiful people with beautiful spirits. You are talking about an amazing moment in time. Now we have movement that goes on and on. Are you ready for the journey to continue? Lol! I know you are! Super Ready! And I'm excited as well to see you around the world just enjoying life, being in peace, feeling grateful, and looking well. I salute your Greatness. And every day, Greater you going to become. And as this journey continues, you will start to experience your own great saying or positive phrases. You may even come up with your own. So here the deal we are making today. I have shared my positivity with you, next time its your turn. Because what I have learn is iron sharpens iron, so there is no reason for us be dull. The Love is in the air

and everyone around me cares. I am determined to win, and positivity is my best of friends.

We Love, We Laugh, We Live

oExpressing yourself helps clear the mind and refreshes the brain.

Here is a few pages for notes

Made in the USA
Columbia, SC
28 February 2021